I got all my sisters with me. We are family, get up everybody and sing! Everyone can see we're
f the people around us they say, can they be that clos   e're
oody and sing! Living life is fun and we've just begun   ghts.
ed, here's what we call our golden rule. Have faith in   t go
oody and sing! We are family, I got all my sisters with   and
e can see we're together, as we walk on by. (FLY!) ar   won't
ne record, we're giving love in a family dose. We are family, I got all my sisters with me. We are
orld's delights. (HIGH!) high hopes we have for the future, and our goal's in sight. (WE!) no we
you won't go wrong, this is our family jewel. We are family, I got all my sisters with me. We are
everybody and sing! We are family, I got all my sisters with me. We are family, get up everybody
ather, I won't tell no lie. (ALL!) all of the people around us they say, can they be that close. Just
n me. We are family, get up everybody and sing! Living life is fun and we've just begun, to get
t. (WE!) no we don't get depressed, here's what we call our golden rule. Have faith in you and
n me. We are family, get up everybody and sing! We are family, I got all my sisters with me. We
up everybody and sing! Everyone can see we're together, as we walk on by. (FLY!) and we fly
e that close. Just let me state for the record, we're giving love in a family dose. We are family, I
begun, to get our share of the world's delights. (HIGH!) high hopes we have for the future, and
n in you and the things you do, you won't go wrong, this is our family jewel. We are family, I got
with me. We are family, get up everybody and sing! We are family, I got all my sisters with me.
!) and we fly just like birds of a feather, I won't tell no lie. (ALL!) all of the people around us they
are family, I got all my sisters with me. We are family, get up everybody and sing! Living life is
r the future, and our goal's in sight. (WE!) no we don't get depressed, here's what we call our
e are family, I got all my sisters with me. We are family, get up everybody and sing! We are fam-
y sisters with me. We are family, get up everybody and sing! Everyone can see we're together,

A gift for:

_____

From:

_____

love notes

WE ARE FAMILY!

CD included featuring Sister Sledge

Photographs by Steve Bloom Images

We are family,

I got all my

sisters with me.

We are family,

get up everyb

ody and sing!

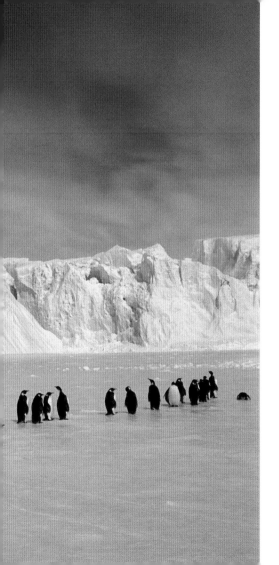

We are family,

I got all my

sisters with me.

We are family,

get up everybody

and sing!

Everyone can

see we're together,

as we **walk** on by.

(FLY!) and we fly just like birds of a feather,

I won't tell no lie.

(ALL!) all of the people around us they say,

can they be

that close.

Just let me state for the record,

we're giving love

in a family dose.

We are family,

I got all my sisters with me.

We are family,

get up everybody and sing!

Living life is fun...

and we've just begun,

to get our share of the

world's delights.

(HIGH!)

high hopes we have for the future,

and our goal's in sight.

here's what we call
our golden rule.

and the things you do, you won't go wrong.

this is our family jewel.

We are family, I got all my sisters with me.

We are family, get up everybody and sing!

We are family, I got all my sisters with me. We are family, get up everybody and sing! We are fa
together, as we walk on by. (FLY!) and we fly just like birds of a feather, I won't tell no lie. (ALL!
giving love in a family dose. We are family, I got all my sisters with me. We are family, get up
(HIGH!) high hopes we have for the future, and our goal's in sight. (WE!) no we don't get dep
wrong, this is our family jewel. We are family, I got all my sisters with me. We are family, get up
sing! We are family, I got all my sisters with me. We are family, get up everybody and sing! Eve
tell no lie. (ALL!) all of the people around us they say, can they be that close. Just let me state
family, get up everybody and sing! Living life is fun and we've just begun, to get our share of t
don't get depressed, here's what we call our golden rule. Have faith in you and the things you
family, get up everybody and sing! We are family, I got all my sisters with me. We are family, ge
and sing! Everyone can see we're together, as we walk on by. (FLY!) and we fly just like birds o
let me state for the record, we're giving love in a family dose. We are family, I got all my sister
our share of the world's delights. (HIGH!) high hopes we have for the future, and our goal's in
the things you do, you won't go wrong, this is our family jewel. We are family, I got all my sister
are family, get up everybody and sing! We are family, I got all my sisters with me. We are famil
just like birds of a feather, I won't tell no lie. (ALL!) all of the people around us they say, can th
got all my sisters with me. We are family, get up everybody and sing! Living life is fun and we've
our goal's in sight. (WE!) no we don't get depressed, here's what we call our golden rule. Have
all my sisters with me. We are family, get up everybody and sing! We are family, I got all my si
We are family, get up everybody and sing! Everyone can see we're together, as we walk on by.
say, can they be that close. Just let me state for the record, we're giving love in a family dose
fun and we've just begun, to get our share of the world's delights. (HIGH!) high hopes we ha
golden rule. Have faith in you and the things you do, you won't go wrong, this is our family jewe
ily, I got all my sisters with me. We are family, get up everybody and sing! We are family, I got